NEW M

GUIDEBOOK

CONFIDENTIAL MATERIAL
IF FOUND PLEASE CONTACT:

NAME: _____

EMAIL: _____

PHONE: _____

HEY THERE!

Congrats on becoming a manager (or leader, supervisor, director... whichever term your organization uses)!

Our goal is to help individuals as they become people managers for the first time. This may mean a promotion in your existing company, or you may have joined a new company in a leadership role. This is for both!

Too often, employees are put into roles without enough direction or resources. This Guidebook is a tool to jumpstart your leadership, including your meetings with other leaders colleagues and team members.

From conversation prompts to space for thoughts and note this is your secret weapon to be confident as you start.

We love hearing from our community! Reach out to us at:
https://managermethod.com/contact

We have plenty of training, tools and resources,
both for managers and employees!

You got this!

Ashley Herd

Founder, Manager Method

TABLE OF CONTENTS

YOU GOT THIS

A few things to remember...

- You earned this role.
- Listen to advice, but decide if it works for you. This is your opportunity.
- You don't have to do it all today.
- If you get overwhelmed, close your eyes and take 10 deep breaths.
- Treat everyone with respect, no matter whether they are "above" or "below" you on the org chart, or what you are speaking with them about.
- Don't just be "open" to new ideas... ask for them.
- Ask questions. And then ask more.
- Listen when people open up to you.
- Take notes (that's where this comes in!)

What made you want this role? Write your thoughts down on the next page so you can turn to them whenever needed.

NOTE TO SELF

(LOOK BACK AT THIS FROM TIME-TO-TIME)

Why did you move into this role? Because you were good at your previous role? Because you wanted a new experience? Write it down!

_____

_____

_____

_____

_____

If you are nervous about leading people, that's normal. What are you fearing will happen?

_____

_____

_____

_____

_____

On the flip side, what are you hoping will happen in your role?

_____

_____

_____

_____

_____

LESSONS LEARNED

Who are great managers or leaders you have had
or known? What made them great?

_____

_____

_____

_____

_____

_____

_____

_____

_____

Flip side again... who are poor managers or
leaders you know? What made them poor?

_____

_____

_____

_____

_____

_____

_____

_____

YOUR OWN PATH

What is your unique value that you are
bringing to the role?

_____

_____

_____

_____

_____

_____

_____

_____

What would success in your role look like?
How would it feel?

_____

_____

_____

_____

_____

_____

_____

_____

_____

ORG CHARTS

WHERE YOU CAN DRAW ORG CHARTS OF THE
COMPANY AND PEOPLE - YOU MAY HAVE THESE
ALREADY (ESPECIALLY IF YOU WERE PROMOTED IN
YOUR CURRENT COMPANY), BUT IT CAN HELP TO
SKETCH THEM OUT.

"MANAGE LIKE A HUMAN" TIP:
*A PERSON'S VALUE SHOULD NOT BE MEASURED BY
THEIR PLACE ON THE ORG CHART.
BUT SOME PEOPLE TREAT THEM THIS WAY.
BE DIFFERENT. TREAT EVERYONE WITH THE SAME
RESPECT, AND PEOPLE WILL REMEMBER.*

YOUR LEADERSHIP

(DRAW YOUR ORG LEADERSHIP CHART -
PEOPLE YOU REPORT TO + OTHERS AT YOUR LEVEL;
INCLUDE TIME ZONES FOR DISPERSED LEADERSHIP)

YOUR TEAM

(DRAW YOUR TEAM STRUCTURE - THE PEOPLE WHO
REPORT TO YOU... AND REPORT TO THEM;
INCLUDE TIME ZONES FOR DISPERSED TEAMS)

YOUR WORLD

(DRAW YOUR DEPARTMENT/OFFICE/COMPANY ORG CHART -
THE DIVISIONS/OFFICES IN YOUR TEAM)

YOUR LEADER

WHERE YOU CAN TAKE NOTES OF HOW YOUR OWN LEADER (OR BOSS/MANAGER) LIKES TO WORK AND WHAT THEY EXPECT.

EVEN IF YOU LEARNED SOME OF THESE IN YOUR INTERVIEW OR WORKED TOGETHER PREVIOUSLY, IT CAN BE HELPFUL TO RECONFIRM AS YOU BEGIN YOUR ROLE.

"MANAGE LIKE A HUMAN" TIP:
SOMETIMES YOU MAY THINK, "I DON'T WANT TO BOTHER THEM." BUT ASKING QUESTIONS OF OTHERS IS A STRENGTH, NOT A WEAKNESS. ASK THEM, AND USE WHAT YOU LEARN TO DEVELOP YOUR OWN LEADERSHIP STYLE.

REMEMBER
(TIPS TO GET STARTED)

IDEALLY, THERE WILL BE ORGANIZATIONAL GOALS AND EACH DEPARTMENT'S/TEAM'S GOALS WILL FLOW FROM THERE. BUT THAT DOESN'T ALWAYS HAPPEN SO SMOOTHLY. EVEN IF NOT, FIND OUT WHAT YOUR BOSS IS TRYING TO ACCOMPLISH, SO YOU CAN LEAD YOUR TEAM IN THE SAME DIRECTION.

YOUR BOSS IS LIKELY GOING TO WANT YOU TO COMMUNICATE MORE AS YOU BEGIN LEADING YOUR TEAM. LET THEM KNOW "LONG-TERM, I WANT TO BE ABLE TO OWN MY TEAM AND MAKE YOUR LIFE EASIER, BUT I ALSO WANT TO ENSURE I GET THE LAY OF THE LAND AS I START. LET ME KNOW WHAT YOU WANT ME TO COME TO YOU WITH, AND I WILL ALSO MAKE SURE TO RAISE QUESTIONS IF I'M IN DOUBT."

IF YOU DON'T CARE FOR YOUR BOSS' STYLE (THAT HAPPENS!), FIND YOUR OWN WAY OF LEADING YOUR TEAM WHILE NOT ALIENATING OR BAD-MOUTHING YOUR BOSS. YOUR TEAM IS LOOKING TO YOU FOR LEADERSHIP, NOT TO BE THEIR BUDDY.

YOUR BOSS MAY WANT "SKIP LEVEL" MEETINGS (WHERE THEY MEET WITH YOUR TEAM MEMBERS INDIVIDUALLY). ENCOURAGE THAT, AND DON'T TELL YOUR TEAM "HEY, DON'T TALK BADLY ABOUT ME!" FOCUS ON BUILDING STRONG, TRUSTING RELATIONSHIPS WITHOUT WORRYING WHAT THEY MAY SAY.

IF YOU EVER HAVE "IMPOSTER SYNDROME," IT CAN BE OKAY TO ASK YOUR BOSS IF THEY EVER FELT THAT WAY. THEY LIKELY HAVE! BEING CANDID CAN HELP YOU GROW.

THESE QUESTIONS ARE EXAMPLES FOR YOU TO ASK AS YOU SEE FIT. YOU MAY (AND LIKELY WILL) HAVE MORE, SO EXTRA NOTES PAGES ARE INCLUDED.

YOUR LEADER
(YOU CAN WRITE THESE IN ONE OR MORE MEETINGS)

NAME: _____

TITLE: _____

PERSONAL DETAILS TO REMEMBER:

_____
_____
_____
_____
_____

LEADERSHIP STYLE:

_____
_____
_____
_____
_____

THEIR GOALS/OBJECTIVES:

_____
_____
_____
_____
_____

YOUR LEADER
(YOU CAN WRITE THESE IN ONE OR MORE MEETINGS)

PET PEEVES:

_____

_____

_____

_____

BUDGET (WHAT YOURS IS AND WHAT
NEEDS APPORVAL):

_____

_____

1:1 MEETING AND UPDATE CADENCE
WITH THEIR FIRST-LINE LEADERS
(HOW & HOW OFTEN DO THEY PREFER
TO MEET/BE UPDATED):

_____

_____

_____

_____

_____

_____

_____

_____

_____

YOUR LEADER

(YOU CAN WRITE THESE IN ONE OR MORE MEETINGS)

WORKING STYLE (NIGHT OWL, ETC.)?

_____

_____

_____

_____

_____

COMMUNICATION PREFERENCES (CALL,
CHAT SLACK, TEXT, SET UP TIME
THROUGH ADMIN, WAIT UNTIL 1:1)?

_____

_____

_____

_____

_____

MANAGING TIME OFF (ANY KEY DATES
TO BE MINDFUL OF FOR YOURSELF
AND YOUR TEAM)?

_____

_____

_____

_____

_____

YOUR LEADER
(YOU CAN WRITE THESE IN ONE OR MORE MEETINGS)

HOW DO THEY DESCRIBE THE CULTURE?

_____
_____
_____
_____
_____

HOW DO THEY INTEGRATE CULTURE
INTO THEIR DAY-TO-DAY?

_____
_____
_____
_____
_____

WHAT IS ADVICE THEY WISH THEY HAD
WHEN THEY BEGAN MANAGING?

_____
_____
_____
_____
_____
_____

YOUR LEADER

IMMEDIATE-TERM NEEDS WHERE MY TEAM AND I CAN DRIVE IMPACT:

_____

_____

_____

_____

_____

_____

_____

_____

_____

LONGER-TERM NEEDS WHERE MY TEAM AND I CAN DRIVE IMPACT:

_____

_____

_____

_____

_____

_____

_____

_____

_____

YOUR LEADER

(EXTRA NOTES PAGES)

YOUR LEADER

(EXTRA NOTES PAGES)

YOUR TEAM
OTHERS' PERSPECTIVES

WHERE YOU CAN TAKE NOTES ABOUT YOUR TEAM
AND HOW TO WORK TOGETHER,
FROM YOUR LEADER AND PEERS.

"MANAGE LIKE A HUMAN" TIP:

*YOUR LEADER AND OTHERS MAY HAVE INPUT
REGARDING YOUR TEAM. LISTEN, BUT GIVE EVERYONE
A FRESH START AS MUCH AS POSSIBLE. DON'T WRITE
ANYONE OFF BEFORE THEY HAVE A CHANCE.*

YOUR TEAM

(AS TOLD BY YOUR LEADER OR COLLEAGUES)

NAME: _____

ROLE: _____

KEY PRIORITIES: _____
_____

ASK THEM ABOUT: _____
_____

OTHER THINGS TO KNOW: _____
_____
_____
_____

NAME: _____

ROLE: _____

KEY PRIORITIES: _____
_____

ASK THEM ABOUT: _____
_____

OTHER THINGS TO KNOW: _____
_____
_____
_____

YOUR TEAM
(AS TOLD BY YOUR LEADER OR COLLEAGUES)

NAME: _____

ROLE: _____

KEY PRIORITIES: _____

_____

ASK THEM ABOUT: _____

_____

OTHER THINGS TO KNOW: _____

_____

_____

_____

NAME: _____

ROLE: _____

KEY PRIORITIES: _____

_____

ASK THEM ABOUT: _____

_____

OTHER THINGS TO KNOW: _____

_____

_____

_____

YOUR TEAM

NAME: _____

ROLE: _____

KEY PRIORITIES: _____
_____

ASK THEM ABOUT: _____
_____

OTHER THINGS TO KNOW: _____
_____
_____
_____

NAME: _____

ROLE: _____

KEY PRIORITIES: _____
_____

ASK THEM ABOUT: _____
_____

OTHER THINGS TO KNOW: _____
_____
_____
_____

YOUR TEAM
(AS TOLD BY YOUR LEADER OR COLLEAGUES)

NAME: _____

ROLE: _____

KEY PRIORITIES: _____
_____

ASK THEM ABOUT: _____
_____

OTHER THINGS TO KNOW: _____
_____
_____
_____

NAME: _____

ROLE: _____

KEY PRIORITIES: _____
_____

ASK THEM ABOUT: _____
_____

OTHER THINGS TO KNOW: _____
_____
_____
_____

YOUR TEAM

(AS TOLD BY YOUR LEADER OR COLLEAGUES)

NAME: _____

ROLE: _____

KEY PRIORITIES: _____

_____

ASK THEM ABOUT: _____

_____

OTHER THINGS TO KNOW: _____

_____

_____

_____

NAME: _____

ROLE: _____

KEY PRIORITIES: _____

_____

ASK THEM ABOUT: _____

_____

OTHER THINGS TO KNOW: _____

_____

_____

_____

YOUR TEAM

(AS TOLD BY YOUR LEADER OR COLLEAGUES)

NAME: _____

ROLE: _____

KEY PRIORITIES: _____

_____

ASK THEM ABOUT: _____

_____

OTHER THINGS TO KNOW: _____

_____

_____

_____

NAME: _____

ROLE: _____

KEY PRIORITIES: _____

_____

ASK THEM ABOUT: _____

_____

OTHER THINGS TO KNOW: _____

_____

_____

_____

YOUR TEAM

NAME: _____

ROLE: _____

KEY PRIORITIES: _____
_____

ASK THEM ABOUT: _____
_____

OTHER THINGS TO KNOW: _____
_____
_____
_____

NAME: _____

ROLE: _____

KEY PRIORITIES: _____
_____

ASK THEM ABOUT: _____
_____

OTHER THINGS TO KNOW: _____
_____
_____
_____

YOUR TEAM
YOUR PERSPECTIVE

WHERE YOU CAN TAKE NOTES ABOUT YOUR TEAM
AND HOW TO WORK TOGETHER,
FROM YOUR OWN MEETINGS WITH THEM.

"MANAGE LIKE A HUMAN" TIP:

YOUR TEAM IS LOOKING TO YOU TO SET THE TONE OF THE RELATIONSHIP. YOUR FIRST CONVERSATIONS SHOULD BE FOCUSED ON LEARNING ABOUT THEM AND THEIR GOALS AND IDEAS. IF YOU JUST TALK ABOUT YOURSELF, THEY WILL REMEMBER.

REMEMBER
(TIPS TO GET STARTED)

- YOU MAY FEEL NERVOUS... AND YOUR EMPLOYEES MAY FEEL THE SAME. IT'S OKAY TO SHARE AND SAY "I'M EXCITED TO LEA THIS TEAM BUT I'M NERVOUS, TOO. IF YOU HAVE ANY QUESTIONS ABOUT HOW I LEAD, PLEASE FEEL FREE TO ASK THEM. I WANT YOUR ADVICE AND INPUT."

- YOU DON'T HAVE TO START BY SHARING ABOUT YOURSELF. YOU CAN SAY, "I'M HAPPY TO ANSWER QUESTIONS YOU HAVE AND GIVE MY BACKGROUND, BUT I WANT TO GET TO KNOW YOU FIRST - YOU, YOUR CAREER AND WHAT'S ON YOUR MIND.

- SOME EMPLOYEES MAY NOT BE EXCITED FOR THEIR NEW BOSS SOME MAY HAVE EVEN INTERVIEWED FOR YOUR ROLE. IF THAT'S THE CASE, IT'S BEST TO BE CANDID, SUCH AS "I KNOW THIS WAS AN OPPORTUNITY YOU WERE CONSIDERED FOR. I MAY BE IN THIS SEAT, BUT I WANT YOU TO HAVE OPPORTUNITIES TO DEVELOP AND BE SEEN, SO YOU ARE READY FOR YOUR NEXT ROLE HERE."

- PART OF THE REASON STANDARD QUESTIONS CAN BE HELPFU IS THAT YOU MAY BE INCLINED TO RELATE TO TEAM MEMBERS WITH YOUR SAME EXPERIENCE ("THEY REMIND ME OF ME!"). BUT YOU WANT ALL TEAM MEMBERS TO FEEL INCLUDED AND THAT THEY ARE BEING TREATED FAIRLY. BE AWARE AS YOU BEGIN LEADING YOUR TEAM IF YOU START TO FAVOR SOME EMPLOYEES.

- THESE INITIAL 1:1 MEETINGS ARE GREAT TO ASK QUESTIONS AND HOLD OFF ON GIVING ADVICE RIGHT AWAY. YOU MAY FEE LIKE YOU ARE "SOLVING" SHORT-TERM ISSUES. BUT FOCUSING MORE ON LISTENING CAN BUILD LONG-TERM TRUST AND SUCCESS.

- THESE MEETINGS CAN BE GOOD TIMES TO SET EXPECTATIONS FOR FUTURE MEETINGS, SUCH AS HAVING A SHARED AGENDA IN ADVANCE, HOW TO PREPARE FOR THE 1:1, ETC.

YOUR TEAM

NAME: _____

ROLE: _____

LOCATION: _____

PERSONAL INFORMATION: _____

_____

_____

KEY CAREER HIGHLIGHTS: _____

_____

_____

_____

CURRENT PRIORITIES: _____

_____

_____

IDEAS FOR TEAM: _____

_____

_____

ADVICE FOR YOU: _____

_____

_____

_____

YOUR TEAM
(NOTES FROM INTRODUCTORY MEETINGS)

NAME: _____

ROLE: _____

LOCATION: _____

PERSONAL INFORMATION: _____

_____

_____

KEY CAREER HIGHLIGHTS: _____

_____

_____

_____

CURRENT PRIORITIES: _____

_____

_____

IDEAS FOR TEAM: _____

_____

_____

ADVICE FOR YOU: _____

_____

_____

_____

YOUR TEAM

(NOTES FROM INTRODUCTORY MEETINGS)

NAME: _____

ROLE: _____

LOCATION: _____

PERSONAL INFORMATION: _____
_____
_____

KEY CAREER HIGHLIGHTS: _____
_____
_____
_____

CURRENT PRIORITIES: _____
_____
_____

IDEAS FOR TEAM: _____
_____
_____

ADVICE FOR YOU: _____
_____
_____

YOUR TEAM

(NOTES FROM INTRODUCTORY MEETINGS)

NAME: _____

ROLE: _____

LOCATION: _____

PERSONAL INFORMATION: _____

_____

_____

KEY CAREER HIGHLIGHTS: _____

_____

_____

_____

CURRENT PRIORITIES: _____

_____

_____

IDEAS FOR TEAM: _____

_____

_____

ADVICE FOR YOU: _____

_____

_____

_____

YOUR TEAM

(NOTES FROM INTRODUCTORY MEETINGS)

NAME: _____

ROLE: _____

LOCATION: _____

PERSONAL INFORMATION: _____

_____

_____

KEY CAREER HIGHLIGHTS: _____

_____

_____

_____

CURRENT PRIORITIES: _____

_____

_____

IDEAS FOR TEAM: _____

_____

_____

ADVICE FOR YOU: _____

_____

_____

_____

YOUR TEAM

(NOTES FROM INTRODUCTORY MEETINGS)

NAME: _____

ROLE: _____

LOCATION: _____

PERSONAL INFORMATION: _____

_____

_____

KEY CAREER HIGHLIGHTS: _____

_____

_____

_____

CURRENT PRIORITIES: _____

_____

_____

IDEAS FOR TEAM: _____

_____

_____

ADVICE FOR YOU: _____

_____

_____

_____

YOUR TEAM

(NOTES FROM INTRODUCTORY MEETINGS)

NAME: _____

ROLE: _____

LOCATION: _____

PERSONAL INFORMATION: _____

_____

_____

KEY CAREER HIGHLIGHTS: _____

_____

_____

_____

CURRENT PRIORITIES: _____

_____

_____

IDEAS FOR TEAM: _____

_____

_____

ADVICE FOR YOU: _____

_____

_____

_____

YOUR TEAM
(NOTES FROM INTRODUCTORY MEETINGS)

NAME: _____

ROLE: _____

LOCATION: _____

PERSONAL INFORMATION: _____
_____
_____

KEY CAREER HIGHLIGHTS: _____
_____
_____
_____

CURRENT PRIORITIES: _____
_____
_____

IDEAS FOR TEAM: _____
_____
_____

ADVICE FOR YOU: _____
_____
_____
_____

YOUR TEAM

(NOTES FROM INTRODUCTORY MEETINGS)

NAME: _____

ROLE: _____

LOCATION: _____

PERSONAL INFORMATION: _____

_____

_____

KEY CAREER HIGHLIGHTS: _____

_____

_____

_____

CURRENT PRIORITIES: _____

_____

_____

IDEAS FOR TEAM: _____

_____

_____

ADVICE FOR YOU: _____

_____

_____

_____

YOUR TEAM

(NOTES FROM INTRODUCTORY MEETINGS)

NAME: _____

ROLE: _____

LOCATION: _____

PERSONAL INFORMATION: _____
_____
_____

KEY CAREER HIGHLIGHTS: _____
_____
_____
_____

CURRENT PRIORITIES: _____
_____
_____

IDEAS FOR TEAM: _____
_____
_____

ADVICE FOR YOU: _____
_____
_____
_____

YOUR TEAM

(NOTES FROM INTRODUCTORY MEETINGS)

NAME: _____

ROLE: _____

LOCATION: _____

PERSONAL INFORMATION: _____

_____

_____

KEY CAREER HIGHLIGHTS: _____

_____

_____

_____

CURRENT PRIORITIES: _____

_____

_____

IDEAS FOR TEAM: _____

_____

_____

ADVICE FOR YOU: _____

_____

_____

YOUR TEAM

(NOTES FROM INTRODUCTORY MEETINGS)

NAME: _____

ROLE: _____

LOCATION: _____

PERSONAL INFORMATION: _____

_____

_____

KEY CAREER HIGHLIGHTS: _____

_____

_____

_____

CURRENT PRIORITIES: _____

_____

_____

IDEAS FOR TEAM: _____

_____

_____

ADVICE FOR YOU: _____

_____

_____

_____

YOUR PEERS & OTHERS

WHERE YOU CAN TAKE NOTES ABOUT OTHER KEY PEOPLE TO KNOW, FROM YOUR LEADER AND PEERS/OTHERS DIRECTLY.

"MANAGING LIKE A HUMAN" TIP:

YOU MAY MEET COLLEAGUES ON OTHER TEAMS WHO YOU WON'T REGULARLY WORK WITH. STILL BUILD RELATIONSHIPS AND BE CURIOUS ABOUT WHAT THEY ARE DOING. IT CAN HELP YOU HAVE A FULL PICTURE AND LEARN, EVEN WHEN YOU LEAST EXPECT IT.

OTHER KEY PEOPLE TO KNOW

(AS TOLD BY YOUR LEADER OR COLLEAGUES)

NAME: _____

DEPARTMENT: _____

ROLE: _____

KEY PRIORITIES: _____

_____

ASK THEM ABOUT: _____

_____

OTHER THINGS TO KNOW: _____

_____

NAME: _____

DEPARTMENT: _____

ROLE: _____

KEY PRIORITIES: _____

_____

ASK THEM ABOUT: _____

_____

OTHER THINGS TO KNOW: _____

_____

OTHER KEY PEOPLE
TO KNOW
(AS TOLD BY YOUR LEADER OR COLLEAGUES)

NAME: _____

DEPARTMENT: _____

ROLE: _____

KEY INITIATVES: _____

_____

ASK THEM ABOUT: _____

_____

OTHER THINGS TO KNOW: _____

_____

NAME: _____

DEPARTMENT: _____

ROLE: _____

KEY INITIATVES: _____

_____

ASK THEM ABOUT: _____

_____

OTHER THINGS TO KNOW: _____

_____

OTHER KEY PEOPLE
TO KNOW
(AS TOLD BY YOUR LEADER OR COLLEAGUES)

NAME: _____

DEPARTMENT: _____

ROLE: _____

KEY INITIATVES: _____

_____

ASK THEM ABOUT: _____

_____

OTHER THINGS TO KNOW: _____

_____

NAME: _____

DEPARTMENT: _____

ROLE: _____

KEY INITIATVES: _____

_____

ASK THEM ABOUT: _____

_____

OTHER THINGS TO KNOW: _____

_____

OTHER KEY PEOPLE
TO KNOW
(AS TOLD BY YOUR LEADER OR COLLEAGUES)

NAME: _____

DEPARTMENT: _____

ROLE: _____

KEY INITIATVES: _____

_____

ASK THEM ABOUT: _____

_____

OTHER THINGS TO KNOW: _____

_____

NAME: _____

DEPARTMENT: _____

ROLE: _____

KEY INITIATVES: _____

_____

ASK THEM ABOUT: _____

_____

OTHER THINGS TO KNOW: _____

_____

OTHER KEY PEOPLE
TO KNOW
(AS TOLD BY YOUR LEADER OR COLLEAGUES)

NAME: _____

DEPARTMENT: _____

ROLE: _____

KEY INITIATVES: _____

_____

ASK THEM ABOUT: _____

_____

OTHER THINGS TO KNOW: _____

_____

NAME: _____

DEPARTMENT: _____

ROLE: _____

KEY INITIATVES: _____

_____

ASK THEM ABOUT: _____

_____

OTHER THINGS TO KNOW: _____

_____

KEY INFO

WHERE YOU CAN TAKE NOTES ABOUT KEY
INFORMATION AND ACROYNMS, FROM YOUR
LEADER, COLLEAGUES AND TEAM.

EVEN IF YOU HAVE WORKED IN THE ORGANIZATION
AS AN INDIVIDUAL CONTRIBUTOR, YOU WILL LIKELY
LEARN NEW SYSTEMS AND ACRONYMS FROM OTHER
LEADERS AND TEAMS.

"MANAGE LIKE A HUMAN" TIP:

*ASK OTHERS "WHAT TOOLS AND REPORTS DO YOU
USE REGULARLY?" YOU (AND YOUR TEAM) CAN OFTEN
LEARN MUCH ABOUT THE COMPANY FROM THESE,
THAT YOU WOULD NOT BE AWARE OF ON YOUR OWN.*

KEY SYSTEMS AND REPORTS
(TECHNOLOGY AND INFO TO LEARN)

NAME: _____

PURPOSE: _____
_____

WHERE LOCATED (WEBSITE/SERVER):
_____
_____

WHO USES IT/THINGS TO KNOW:
_____
_____
_____
_____
_____

NAME: _____

PURPOSE: _____
_____

WHERE LOCATED (WEBSITE/SERVER):
_____
_____

WHO USES IT/THINGS TO KNOW:
_____
_____
_____
_____
_____

KEY SYSTEMS AND REPORTS
(TECHNOLOGY AND INFO TO LEARN)

NAME: _____

PURPOSE: _____
_____

WHERE LOCATED (WEBSITE/SERVER):
_____
_____

WHO USES IT/THINGS TO KNOW:
_____
_____
_____
_____
_____

NAME: _____

PURPOSE: _____
_____

WHERE LOCATED (WEBSITE/SERVER):
_____
_____

WHO USES IT/THINGS TO KNOW:
_____
_____
_____
_____
_____

KEY SYSTEMS AND REPORTS
(TECHNOLOGY AND INFO TO LEARN)

NAME: _____

PURPOSE: _____

_____

WHERE LOCATED (WEBSITE/SERVER):

_____

_____

WHO USES IT/THINGS TO KNOW:

_____

_____

_____

_____

_____

NAME: _____

PURPOSE: _____

_____

WHERE LOCATED (WEBSITE/SERVER):

_____

_____

WHO USES IT/THINGS TO KNOW:

_____

_____

_____

_____

_____

ACRONYMS
(EVERY COMPANY AND TEAM HAS THEM)

ACRONYM: MEANING::

_____   _____
_____   _____
_____   _____
_____   _____
_____   _____
_____   _____
_____   _____
_____   _____
_____   _____
_____   _____
_____   _____
_____   _____
_____   _____
_____   _____
_____   _____
_____   _____
_____   _____
_____   _____
_____   _____
_____   _____
_____   _____
_____   _____
_____   _____
_____   _____

GOALS & PROJECTS

WHERE YOU CAN TAKE NOTES ABOUT YOUR 30/60/90 GOALS AND YOUR TEAM'S PROJECTS, FROM YOUR LEADER AND OTHERS.

"MANAGE LIKE A HUMAN" TIP:

YOU ARE NOT HIRED TO BE THE EXPERT IN EVERYTHING, BUT TO LEAD A TEAM OF EXPERTS. FIND OUT HOW MUCH YOU ARE EXPECTED TO KNOW, AND LET YOUR TEAM DRIVE ACTION.

30/60/90 DAY GOALS
(TEAM-RELATED, MEETING OTHERS, ETC.)

30 DAYS: _____

_____

_____

_____

_____

_____

_____

_____

60 DAYS: _____

_____

_____

_____

_____

_____

_____

_____

90 DAYS: _____

_____

_____

_____

_____

_____

_____

_____

KEY PROJECTS
(WHAT YOUR TEAM IS TACKLING NOW)

NAME/DESCRIPTION: _____

DETAILS/OWNERS: _____

_____

_____

_____

_____

OBJECTIVES & DEADLINES: _____

_____

_____

_____

_____

NOTES: _____

_____

_____

_____

_____

_____

_____

_____

_____

_____

_____

_____

KEY PROJECTS
(WHAT YOUR TEAM IS TACKLING NOW)

NAME/DESCRIPTION: _____

DETAILS/OWNERS: _____
_____
_____
_____
_____

OBJECTIVES & DEADLINES: _____
_____
_____
_____
_____
_____

NOTES: _____
_____
_____
_____
_____
_____
_____
_____
_____
_____
_____
_____
_____

KEY PROJECTS
(WHAT YOUR TEAM IS TACKLING NOW)

NAME/DESCRIPTION: _____

DETAILS/OWNERS: _____

_____

_____

_____

_____

OBJECTIVES & DEADLINES: _____

_____

_____

_____

_____

_____

NOTES: _____

_____

_____

_____

_____

_____

_____

_____

_____

_____

_____

KEY PROJECTS
(WHAT YOUR TEAM IS TACKLING NOW)

NAME/DESCRIPTION: _____

DETAILS/OWNERS: _____

_____

_____

_____

_____

OBJECTIVES & DEADLINES: _____

_____

_____

_____

_____

_____

NOTES: _____

_____

_____

_____

_____

_____

_____

_____

_____

_____

_____

_____

_____

KEY PROJECTS
(WHAT YOUR TEAM IS TACKLING NOW)

NAME/DESCRIPTION: _____

DETAILS/OWNERS: _____

_____

_____

_____

_____

OBJECTIVES & DEADLINES: _____

_____

_____

_____

_____

_____

NOTES: _____

_____

_____

_____

_____

_____

_____

_____

_____

_____

_____

_____

KEY PROJECTS
(WHAT YOUR TEAM IS TACKLING NOW)

NAME/DESCRIPTION: _____

DETAILS/OWNERS: _____

_____

_____

_____

_____

OBJECTIVES & DEADLINES: _____

_____

_____

_____

_____

_____

NOTES: _____

_____

_____

_____

_____

_____

_____

_____

_____

_____

_____

_____

KEY PROJECTS
(WHAT YOUR TEAM IS TACKLING NOW)

NAME/DESCRIPTION: _____

DETAILS/OWNERS: _____

_____

_____

_____

_____

OBJECTIVES & DEADLINES: _____

_____

_____

_____

_____

_____

NOTES: _____

_____

_____

_____

_____

_____

_____

_____

_____

_____

_____

_____

KEY PROJECTS
(WHAT YOUR TEAM IS TACKLING NOW)

NAME/DESCRIPTION: _____

DETAILS/OWNERS: _____

_____

_____

_____

_____

OBJECTIVES & DEADLINES: _____

_____

_____

_____

_____

_____

NOTES: _____

_____

_____

_____

_____

_____

_____

_____

_____

_____

_____

_____

MEETING NOTES
YOUR LEADER - 1:1

WHERE YOU CAN TAKE NOTES ABOUT
YOUR 1:1 MEETINGS WITH YOUR LEADER.

"MANAGE LIKE A HUMAN" TIP:

*AS YOU DEVELOP A RELATIONSHIP WITH YOUR OWN
LEADER, KEEP ASKING QUESTIONS AND FRAME YOUR
MEETINGS AROUND THE ORGANIZATION'S AND YOUR
LEADER'S GOALS TO ENSURE YOURS CASCADE DOWN.*

1:1 MEETING NOTES
(MEETINGS WITH YOUR BOSS/LEADER)

DATE: _____

LEADER'S CURRENT GOALS (RELATED TO YOUR
TEAM OR NOT): _____

_____

_____

ITEMS TO DISCUSS (WHERE YOU/YOUR TEAM
NEED ADVICE/SUPPORT):

_____

_____

_____

_____

_____

NOTES: _____

_____

_____

_____

_____

_____

_____

_____

MY ACTION ITEMS (TO-DO'S) & DEADLINES:

_____

_____

_____

_____

1:1 MEETING NOTES
(MEETINGS WITH YOUR BOSS/LEADER)

DATE: _____

LEADER'S CURRENT GOALS (RELATED TO YOUR
TEAM OR NOT): _____

_____

_____

ITEMS TO DISCUSS (WHERE YOU/YOUR TEAM
NEED ADVICE/SUPPORT):

_____

_____

_____

_____

_____

NOTES:_____

_____

_____

_____

_____

_____

_____

_____

MY ACTION ITEMS (TO-DO'S) & DEADLINES:

_____

_____

_____

_____

1:1 MEETING NOTES
(MEETINGS WITH YOUR BOSS/LEADER)

DATE: _____

LEADER'S CURRENT GOALS (RELATED TO YOUR TEAM OR NOT): _____

_____

_____

ITEMS TO DISCUSS (WHERE YOU/YOUR TEAM NEED ADVICE/SUPPORT):

_____

_____

_____

_____

_____

NOTES:_____

_____

_____

_____

_____

_____

_____

_____

MY ACTION ITEMS (TO-DO'S) & DEADLINES:

_____

_____

_____

_____

1:1 MEETING NOTES
(MEETINGS WITH YOUR BOSS/LEADER)

DATE: _____

LEADER'S CURRENT GOALS (RELATED TO YOUR TEAM OR NOT): _____

_____

_____

ITEMS TO DISCUSS (WHERE YOU/YOUR TEAM NEED ADVICE/SUPPORT):

_____

_____

_____

_____

_____

NOTES: _____

_____

_____

_____

_____

_____

_____

_____

MY ACTION ITEMS (TO-DO'S) & DEADLINES:

_____

_____

_____

_____

1:1 MEETING NOTES
(MEETINGS WITH YOUR BOSS/LEADER)

DATE: _____

LEADER'S CURRENT GOALS (RELATED TO YOUR TEAM OR NOT): _____
_____
_____

ITEMS TO DISCUSS (WHERE YOU/YOUR TEAM NEED ADVICE/SUPPORT):
_____
_____
_____
_____
_____

NOTES:_____
_____
_____
_____
_____
_____
_____
_____

MY ACTION ITEMS (TO-DO'S) & DEADLINES:
_____
_____
_____
_____

1:1 MEETING NOTES
(MEETINGS WITH YOUR BOSS/LEADER)

DATE: _____

LEADER'S CURRENT GOALS (RELATED TO YOUR TEAM OR NOT): _____

_____

_____

ITEMS TO DISCUSS (WHERE YOU/YOUR TEAM NEED ADVICE/SUPPORT):

_____

_____

_____

_____

_____

NOTES:_____

_____

_____

_____

_____

_____

_____

_____

MY ACTION ITEMS (TO-DO'S) & DEADLINES:

_____

_____

_____

_____

1:1 MEETING NOTES
(MEETINGS WITH YOUR BOSS/LEADER)

DATE: _____

LEADER'S CURRENT GOALS (RELATED TO YOUR
TEAM OR NOT): _____

_____

_____

ITEMS TO DISCUSS (WHERE YOU/YOUR TEAM
NEED ADVICE/SUPPORT):

_____

_____

_____

_____

_____

NOTES:_____

_____

_____

_____

_____

_____

_____

_____

_____

MY ACTION ITEMS (TO-DO'S) & DEADLINES:

_____

_____

_____

_____

1:1 MEETING NOTES
(MEETINGS WITH YOUR BOSS/LEADER)

DATE: _____

LEADER'S CURRENT GOALS (RELATED TO YOUR
TEAM OR NOT): _____

_____

_____

ITEMS TO DISCUSS (WHERE YOU/YOUR TEAM
NEED ADVICE/SUPPORT):

_____

_____

_____

_____

_____

NOTES:_____

_____

_____

_____

_____

_____

_____

_____

MY ACTION ITEMS (TO-DO'S) & DEADLINES:

_____

_____

_____

_____

1:1 MEETING NOTES
(MEETINGS WITH YOUR BOSS/LEADER)

DATE: _____

LEADER'S CURRENT GOALS (RELATED TO YOUR
TEAM OR NOT): _____

_____

_____

ITEMS TO DISCUSS (WHERE YOU/YOUR TEAM
NEED ADVICE/SUPPORT):

_____

_____

_____

_____

NOTES: _____

_____

_____

_____

_____

_____

_____

_____

MY ACTION ITEMS (TO-DO'S) & DEADLINES:

_____

_____

_____

_____

1:1 MEETING NOTES
(MEETINGS WITH YOUR BOSS/LEADER)

DATE: _____

LEADER'S CURRENT GOALS (RELATED TO YOUR
TEAM OR NOT): _____

_____

_____

ITEMS TO DISCUSS (WHERE YOU/YOUR TEAM
NEED ADVICE/SUPPORT):

_____

_____

_____

_____

_____

NOTES:_____

_____

_____

_____

_____

_____

_____

_____

MY ACTION ITEMS (TO-DO'S) & DEADLINES:

_____

_____

_____

_____

1:1 MEETING NOTES
(MEETINGS WITH YOUR BOSS/LEADER)

DATE: _____

LEADER'S CURRENT GOALS (RELATED TO YOUR
TEAM OR NOT): _____

_____

_____

ITEMS TO DISCUSS (WHERE YOU/YOUR TEAM
NEED ADVICE/SUPPORT):

_____

_____

_____

_____

_____

NOTES:_____

_____

_____

_____

_____

_____

_____

_____

_____

MY ACTION ITEMS (TO-DO'S) & DEADLINES:

_____

_____

_____

_____

1:1 MEETING NOTES
(MEETINGS WITH YOUR BOSS/LEADER)

DATE: _____

LEADER'S CURRENT GOALS (RELATED TO YOUR
TEAM OR NOT): _____

_____

_____

ITEMS TO DISCUSS (WHERE YOU/YOUR TEAM
NEED ADVICE/SUPPORT):

_____

_____

_____

_____

_____

NOTES:_____

_____

_____

_____

_____

_____

_____

_____

MY ACTION ITEMS (TO-DO'S) & DEADLINES:

_____

_____

_____

_____

1:1 MEETING NOTES
(MEETINGS WITH YOUR BOSS/LEADER)

DATE: _____

LEADER'S CURRENT GOALS (RELATED TO YOUR
TEAM OR NOT): _____

_____

_____

ITEMS TO DISCUSS (WHERE YOU/YOUR TEAM
NEED ADVICE/SUPPORT):

_____

_____

_____

_____

_____

NOTES: _____

_____

_____

_____

_____

_____

_____

_____

MY ACTION ITEMS (TO-DO'S) & DEADLINES:

_____

_____

_____

_____

1:1 MEETING NOTES
(MEETINGS WITH YOUR BOSS/LEADER)

DATE: _____

LEADER'S CURRENT GOALS (RELATED TO YOUR TEAM OR NOT): _____

_____

_____

ITEMS TO DISCUSS (WHERE YOU/YOUR TEAM NEED ADVICE/SUPPORT):

_____

_____

_____

_____

_____

NOTES: _____

_____

_____

_____

_____

_____

_____

_____

MY ACTION ITEMS (TO-DO'S) & DEADLINES:

_____

_____

_____

_____

1:1 MEETING NOTES
(MEETINGS WITH YOUR BOSS/LEADER)

DATE: _____

LEADER'S CURRENT GOALS (RELATED TO YOUR
TEAM OR NOT): _____

_____

_____

ITEMS TO DISCUSS (WHERE YOU/YOUR TEAM
NEED ADVICE/SUPPORT):

_____

_____

_____

_____

_____

NOTES: _____

_____

_____

_____

_____

_____

_____

_____

MY ACTION ITEMS (TO-DO'S) & DEADLINES:

_____

_____

_____

_____

1:1 MEETING NOTES
(MEETINGS WITH YOUR BOSS/LEADER)

DATE: _____

LEADER'S CURRENT GOALS (RELATED TO YOUR
TEAM OR NOT): _____

_____

_____

ITEMS TO DISCUSS (WHERE YOU/YOUR TEAM
NEED ADVICE/SUPPORT):

_____

_____

_____

_____

_____

NOTES: _____

_____

_____

_____

_____

_____

_____

_____

MY ACTION ITEMS (TO-DO'S) & DEADLINES:

_____

_____

_____

_____

MEETING NOTES
YOUR TEAM - GROUP

WHERE YOU CAN TAKE NOTES ABOUT
YOUR LARGER TEAM MEETINGS.

"MANAGE LIKE A HUMAN" TIP:

IN YOUR TEAM MEETINGS, SOLICIT INPUT FROM SOME OF THE QUIETER TEAM MEMBERS WHO MAY NOT BE AS VOCAL. WHEN TEAMS ASK QUESTIONS, ASK OTHERS FOR THEIR IDEAS BEFORE GIVING YOURS.

REMEMBER
(TIPS TO GET STARTED)

- A BEST PRACTICE CAN BE TO HAVE TEAM MEETINGS AT THE BEGINNING OF THE WEEK (E.G., MONDAY MORNING) BEFORE THE WEEK GETS HECTIC. THIS CAN ALSO MAKE YOUR 1:1 MEETINGS WITH YOUR TEAM MORE VALUABLE, BECAUSE YOU CAN FOLLOW UP ON ANY TOPICS FROM TH TEAM MEETING.

- IF YOUR TEAM IS SPREAD ACROSS MULTIPLE TIME ZONES, DON'T JUST MAKE ONE GROUP BEAR THE BURDEN. TAKE TURNS AND ROTATE SCHEDULES TO MAKE SURE IT IS FAIR

- IF YOUR TEAM IS SO SPREAD OUT GLOBALLY THAT IT IS ESPECIALLY CHALLENGING TO HAVE WEEKLY MEETINGS, CONSIDER DIVIDING THE TEAM INTO 2+ GROUPS. HAVE WEEKLY MEETINGS WITH THOSE, AND WHOLE-TEAM MEETINGS MONTHLY OR QUARTERLY.

- AS YOU BEGIN IN ROLE, SHOW YOU ARE LISTENING. KEEP THE FOCUS ON THE EMPLOYEES. ASK HOW MEETINGS HAVE BEEN RUN, AND ANY INPUT THEY WOULD HAVE ON WHAT WORKS/NEEDS ADJUSTMENT.

- QUESTIONS TO ASK DURING YOUR TEAM:
  - KEY WINS SINCE LAST MEETING
  - LESSONS LEARNED
  - WHERE ARE YOU BLOCKED?
  - GOALS FOR THE WEEK

- A BEST PRACTICE IS TO GIVE YOUR TEAM MEMBERS THE OPPORTUNITY TO "OWN" THE MEETING, INCLUDING ADDING AGENDA ITEMS AND IDEAS DURING THEIR TURN. YOU CAN TALK THROUGH IT WITH THEM IN THEIR 1:1 BEFORE THE TEAM MEETING SO THAT THEY FEEL PREPARED.

TEAM MEETING NOTES
(GROUP)

DATE: _____

NOTES: _____

_____

_____

_____

_____

_____

_____

_____

_____

_____

_____

TEAM'S ACTION ITEMS & DEADLINES:

_____

_____

_____

_____

_____

MY FOLLOW UP (SUPPORT/1:1 TOPICS):

_____

_____

_____

_____

_____

TEAM MEETING NOTES
(GROUP)

DATE: _____

NOTES: _____

_____

_____

_____

_____

_____

_____

_____

_____

_____

_____

TEAM'S ACTION ITEMS & DEADLINES:

_____

_____

_____

_____

_____

MY FOLLOW UP (SUPPORT/1:1 TOPICS):

_____

_____

_____

_____

_____

TEAM MEETING NOTES
(GROUP)

DATE: _____

NOTES: _____

_____

_____

_____

_____

_____

_____

_____

_____

_____

_____

TEAM'S ACTION ITEMS & DEADLINES:

_____

_____

_____

_____

_____

MY FOLLOW UP (SUPPORT/1:1 TOPICS):

_____

_____

_____

_____

_____

TEAM MEETING NOTES
(GROUP)

DATE: _____

NOTES: _____

_____

_____

_____

_____

_____

_____

_____

_____

_____

_____

_____

TEAM'S ACTION ITEMS & DEADLINES:

_____

_____

_____

_____

_____

MY FOLLOW UP (SUPPORT/1:1 TOPICS):

_____

_____

_____

_____

_____

TEAM MEETING NOTES
(GROUP)

DATE: _____

NOTES: _____

_____

_____

_____

_____

_____

_____

_____

_____

_____

_____

_____

TEAM'S ACTION ITEMS & DEADLINES:

_____

_____

_____

_____

_____

MY FOLLOW UP (SUPPORT/1:1 TOPICS):

_____

_____

_____

_____

_____

_____

TEAM MEETING NOTES
(GROUP)

DATE: _____

NOTES: _____

_____

_____

_____

_____

_____

_____

_____

_____

_____

_____

TEAM'S ACTION ITEMS & DEADLINES:

_____

_____

_____

_____

MY FOLLOW UP (SUPPORT/1:1 TOPICS):

_____

_____

_____

_____

TEAM MEETING NOTES
(GROUP)

DATE: _____

NOTES: _____

_____
_____
_____
_____
_____
_____
_____
_____
_____
_____

TEAM'S ACTION ITEMS & DEADLINES:

_____
_____
_____
_____
_____

MY FOLLOW UP (SUPPORT/1:1 TOPICS):

_____
_____
_____
_____
_____

TEAM MEETING NOTES
(GROUP)

DATE: _____

NOTES: _____

_____

_____

_____

_____

_____

_____

_____

_____

_____

_____

TEAM'S ACTION ITEMS & DEADLINES:

_____

_____

_____

_____

_____

MY FOLLOW UP (SUPPORT/1:1 TOPICS):

_____

_____

_____

_____

_____

TEAM MEETING NOTES

(GROUP)

DATE: _____

NOTES: _____

_____

_____

_____

_____

_____

_____

_____

_____

_____

_____

TEAM'S ACTION ITEMS & DEADLINES:

_____

_____

_____

_____

_____

MY FOLLOW UP (SUPPORT/1:1 TOPICS):

_____

_____

_____

_____

_____

TEAM MEETING NOTES
(GROUP)

DATE: _____

NOTES: _____

_____

_____

_____

_____

_____

_____

_____

_____

_____

TEAM'S ACTION ITEMS & DEADLINES:

_____

_____

_____

_____

_____

MY FOLLOW UP (SUPPORT/1:1 TOPICS):

_____

_____

_____

_____

_____

TEAM MEETING NOTES
(GROUP)

DATE: _____

NOTES: _____

_____

_____

_____

_____

_____

_____

_____

_____

_____

_____

TEAM'S ACTION ITEMS & DEADLINES:

_____

_____

_____

_____

_____

MY FOLLOW UP (SUPPORT/1:1 TOPICS):

_____

_____

_____

_____

_____

TEAM MEETING NOTES
(GROUP)

DATE: _____

NOTES: _____

_____

_____

_____

_____

_____

_____

_____

_____

_____

_____

TEAM'S ACTION ITEMS & DEADLINES:

_____

_____

_____

_____

_____

MY FOLLOW UP (SUPPORT/1:1 TOPICS):

_____

_____

_____

_____

_____

TEAM MEETING NOTES

(GROUP)

DATE: _____

NOTES: _____

_____

_____

_____

_____

_____

_____

_____

_____

_____

_____

TEAM'S ACTION ITEMS & DEADLINES:

_____

_____

_____

_____

_____

MY FOLLOW UP (SUPPORT/1:1 TOPICS):

_____

_____

_____

_____

_____

TEAM MEETING NOTES
(GROUP)

DATE: _____

NOTES: _____

_____

_____

_____

_____

_____

_____

_____

_____

_____

_____

TEAM'S ACTION ITEMS & DEADLINES:

_____

_____

_____

_____

_____

MY FOLLOW UP (SUPPORT/1:1 TOPICS):

_____

_____

_____

_____

_____

TEAM MEETING NOTES

(GROUP)

DATE: _____

NOTES: _____

_____

_____

_____

_____

_____

_____

_____

_____

_____

_____

TEAM'S ACTION ITEMS & DEADLINES:

_____

_____

_____

_____

_____

MY FOLLOW UP (SUPPORT/1:1 TOPICS):

_____

_____

_____

_____

_____

TEAM MEETING NOTES
(GROUP)

DATE: _____

NOTES: _____

_____
_____
_____
_____
_____
_____
_____
_____
_____
_____
_____

TEAM'S ACTION ITEMS & DEADLINES:

_____
_____
_____
_____
_____

MY FOLLOW UP (SUPPORT/1:1 TOPICS):

_____
_____
_____
_____
_____

MEETING NOTES
YOUR TEAM - 1:1

WHERE YOU CAN TAKE NOTES ABOUT
YOUR 1:1 MEETINGS WITH YOUR TEAM.

"MANAGE LIKE A HUMAN" TIP:

*WORK TOGETHER WITH YOUR TEAM TO BUILD THE
AGENDAS FOR YOUR 1:1 MEETINGS, SO THAT THEY
ARE IDENTIFYING THEIR CHALLENGES AND GETTING
YOUR HELP, AND YOU ARE GETTING THEIR INPUT AND
DRIVING THEIR DEVELOPMENT*

REMEMBER

(TIPS TO GET STARTED)

- BY HAVING YOUR TEAM MEETINGS TO START THE WEEK, YOU CAN USE ANY INSIGHTS/ACTION ITEMS FROM THOSE TO HELP FRAME YOUR 1:1 MEETINGS.

- HONOR YOUR 1:1 MEETING TIMES. IF YOU ARE DONE EARLY, YOU CAN ALWAYS GIVE TIME BACK. BUT FREQUENTLY CANCELLING, MISSING OR RESCHEDULING YOUR 1:1 MEETINGS SENDS A MESSAGE THAT YOU DON'T CARE ABOUT YOUR EMPLOYEES.

- YOUR 1:1 MEETINGS WITH YOUR REPORTS SHOULD BE PRIMARILY FOR THEIR BENEFIT. THAT CAN MEAN THAT THEY DRIVE THE AGENDA AND RAISE THEIR OWN CHALLENGES, IT CAN ALSO MEAN YOU HAVING PRIVATE COACHING CONVERSATIONS THAT WOULD NOT BE APPROPRIATE IN A TEAM SETTING.

- THESE COACHING CONVERSATIONS CAN BE AROUND SPECIFIC PERFORMANCE ("HEY, LET'S WALK THROUGH YOUR DECK AND TALK THROUGH SO I CAN UNDERSTAND AND GIVE FEEDBACK" OR "I KNOW I MADE A LOT OF EDITS, AND I WANT YOU TO UNDERSTAND THEM AND TALK THROUGH EACH OF THEM.").

- THEY CAN ALSO BE OPEN-ENDED CONVERSATIONS BASED ON YOUR OBSERVATIONS ("I NOTICED YOU SEEMED MORE QUIET THAN NORMAL THIS MORNING. IS EVERYTHING OKAY?").

- SET EXPECTATIONS AROUND 1:1 MEETINGS SO THAT THEY ARE PRODUCTIVE. THIS CAN INCLUDE:
  - AGENDA SET IN ADVANCE
  - COLLABORATIVE AGENDA (AN OKR SOFTWARE OR SHARED GOOGLE DOC/ONENOTE NOTEBOOK/NOTION PAGE)
  - WRITING DOWN ACTION ITEMS SO THAT YOU ARE BUILDING THE NEXT WEEK'S AGENDA DURING YOUR MEETING

- YOU CAN END MEETINGS BY ASKING "WHAT ELSE?" - IT'S OKAY IF A TOPIC THAT COMES UP THAT WAS NOT ON THE AGENDA.

1:1 MEETING NOTES
(MEETINGS WITH YOUR REPORTS)

NAME: _____ DATE: _____

ITEMS TO DISCUSS (FEEDBACK/SUPPORT):

_____

_____

_____

_____

NOTES: _____

_____

_____

_____

FEEDBACK/ACTIONS FOR YOU:

_____

_____

_____

NAME: _____ DATE: _____

ITEMS TO DISCUSS (FEEDBACK/SUPPORT):

_____

_____

_____

_____

NOTES: _____

_____

_____

_____

FEEDBACK/ACTIONS FOR YOU:

_____

_____

_____

1:1 MEETING NOTES
(MEETINGS WITH YOUR REPORTS)

NAME: _____ DATE: _____

ITEMS TO DISCUSS (FEEDBACK/SUPPORT):

_____

_____

_____

_____

NOTES: _____

_____

_____

_____

FEEDBACK/ACTIONS FOR YOU:

_____

_____

_____

NAME: _____ DATE: _____

ITEMS TO DISCUSS (FEEDBACK/SUPPORT):

_____

_____

_____

_____

NOTES: _____

_____

_____

_____

FEEDBACK/ACTIONS FOR YOU:

_____

_____

_____

1:1 MEETING NOTES
(MEETINGS WITH YOUR REPORTS)

NAME: _____ DATE: _____

ITEMS TO DISCUSS (FEEDBACK/SUPPORT):

_____

_____

_____

_____

NOTES: _____

_____

_____

_____

FEEDBACK/ACTIONS FOR YOU:

_____

_____

_____

NAME: _____ DATE: _____

ITEMS TO DISCUSS (FEEDBACK/SUPPORT):

_____

_____

_____

_____

NOTES: _____

_____

_____

_____

FEEDBACK/ACTIONS FOR YOU:

_____

_____

_____

1:1 MEETING NOTES
(MEETINGS WITH YOUR REPORTS)

NAME: _____ DATE: _____

ITEMS TO DISCUSS (FEEDBACK/SUPPORT):

_____

_____

_____

_____

NOTES: _____

_____

_____

_____

FEEDBACK/ACTIONS FOR YOU:

_____

_____

_____

NAME: _____ DATE: _____

ITEMS TO DISCUSS (FEEDBACK/SUPPORT):

_____

_____

_____

_____

NOTES: _____

_____

_____

_____

FEEDBACK/ACTIONS FOR YOU:

_____

_____

_____

1:1 MEETING NOTES
(MEETINGS WITH YOUR REPORTS)

NAME: _____ DATE: _____

ITEMS TO DISCUSS (FEEDBACK/SUPPORT):

_____

_____

_____

_____

NOTES: _____

_____

_____

_____

FEEDBACK/ACTIONS FOR YOU:

_____

_____

_____

NAME: _____ DATE: _____

ITEMS TO DISCUSS (FEEDBACK/SUPPORT):

_____

_____

_____

_____

NOTES: _____

_____

_____

_____

FEEDBACK/ACTIONS FOR YOU:

_____

_____

_____

1:1 MEETING NOTES
(MEETINGS WITH YOUR REPORTS)

NAME: _____   DATE: _____

ITEMS TO DISCUSS (FEEDBACK/SUPPORT):

_____
_____
_____
_____

NOTES:

_____
_____
_____
_____

FEEDBACK/ACTIONS FOR YOU:

_____
_____
_____

NAME: _____   DATE: _____

ITEMS TO DISCUSS (FEEDBACK/SUPPORT):

_____
_____
_____
_____

NOTES:

_____
_____
_____
_____

FEEDBACK/ACTIONS FOR YOU:

_____
_____
_____

1:1 MEETING NOTES
(MEETINGS WITH YOUR REPORTS)

NAME: _____ DATE: _____

ITEMS TO DISCUSS (FEEDBACK/SUPPORT):

_____
_____
_____
_____

NOTES: _____

_____
_____
_____

FEEDBACK/ACTIONS FOR YOU:

_____
_____
_____

NAME: _____ DATE: _____

ITEMS TO DISCUSS (FEEDBACK/SUPPORT):

_____
_____
_____
_____

NOTES: _____

_____
_____
_____

FEEDBACK/ACTIONS FOR YOU:

_____
_____
_____

1:1 MEETING NOTES
(MEETINGS WITH YOUR REPORTS)

NAME: _____ DATE: _____

ITEMS TO DISCUSS (FEEDBACK/SUPPORT):

_____

_____

_____

_____

NOTES: _____

_____

_____

_____

FEEDBACK/ACTIONS FOR YOU:

_____

_____

_____

NAME: _____ DATE: _____

ITEMS TO DISCUSS (FEEDBACK/SUPPORT):

_____

_____

_____

_____

NOTES: _____

_____

_____

_____

FEEDBACK/ACTIONS FOR YOU:

_____

_____

_____

1:1 MEETING NOTES
(MEETINGS WITH YOUR REPORTS)

NAME: _____ DATE: _____

ITEMS TO DISCUSS (FEEDBACK/SUPPORT):

_____

_____

_____

_____

NOTES: _____

_____

_____

_____

FEEDBACK/ACTIONS FOR YOU:

_____

_____

_____

NAME: _____ DATE: _____

ITEMS TO DISCUSS (FEEDBACK/SUPPORT):

_____

_____

_____

_____

NOTES: _____

_____

_____

_____

FEEDBACK/ACTIONS FOR YOU:

_____

_____

_____

1:1 MEETING NOTES
(MEETINGS WITH YOUR REPORTS)

NAME: _____ DATE: _____

ITEMS TO DISCUSS (FEEDBACK/SUPPORT):

_____
_____
_____
_____

NOTES: _____

_____
_____
_____

FEEDBACK/ACTIONS FOR YOU:

_____
_____
_____

NAME: _____ DATE: _____

ITEMS TO DISCUSS (FEEDBACK/SUPPORT):

_____
_____
_____
_____

NOTES: _____

_____
_____
_____

FEEDBACK/ACTIONS FOR YOU:

_____
_____
_____

1:1 MEETING NOTES
(MEETINGS WITH YOUR REPORTS)

NAME: _____ DATE: _____

ITEMS TO DISCUSS (FEEDBACK/SUPPORT):

_____

_____

_____

_____

NOTES: _____

_____

_____

_____

FEEDBACK/ACTIONS FOR YOU:

_____

_____

_____

NAME: _____ DATE: _____

ITEMS TO DISCUSS (FEEDBACK/SUPPORT):

_____

_____

_____

_____

NOTES: _____

_____

_____

_____

FEEDBACK/ACTIONS FOR YOU:

_____

_____

_____

1:1 MEETING NOTES
(MEETINGS WITH YOUR REPORTS)

NAME: _____ DATE: _____

ITEMS TO DISCUSS (FEEDBACK/SUPPORT):

_____

_____

_____

_____

NOTES: _____

_____

_____

_____

FEEDBACK/ACTIONS FOR YOU:

_____

_____

_____

NAME: _____ DATE: _____

ITEMS TO DISCUSS (FEEDBACK/SUPPORT):

_____

_____

_____

_____

NOTES: _____

_____

_____

_____

FEEDBACK/ACTIONS FOR YOU:

_____

_____

_____

1:1 MEETING NOTES
(MEETINGS WITH YOUR REPORTS)

NAME: _____ DATE: _____

ITEMS TO DISCUSS (FEEDBACK/SUPPORT):

_____

_____

_____

_____

NOTES: _____

_____

_____

_____

FEEDBACK/ACTIONS FOR YOU:

_____

_____

_____

NAME: _____ DATE: _____

ITEMS TO DISCUSS (FEEDBACK/SUPPORT):

_____

_____

_____

_____

NOTES: _____

_____

_____

_____

FEEDBACK/ACTIONS FOR YOU:

_____

_____

_____

1:1 MEETING NOTES
(MEETINGS WITH YOUR REPORTS)

NAME: _____ DATE: _____

ITEMS TO DISCUSS (FEEDBACK/SUPPORT):

_____
_____
_____
_____

NOTES: _____

_____
_____
_____

FEEDBACK/ACTIONS FOR YOU:

_____
_____
_____

NAME: _____ DATE: _____

ITEMS TO DISCUSS (FEEDBACK/SUPPORT):

_____
_____
_____
_____

NOTES: _____

_____
_____
_____

FEEDBACK/ACTIONS FOR YOU:

_____
_____
_____

1:1 MEETING NOTES
(MEETINGS WITH YOUR REPORTS)

NAME: _____ DATE: _____

ITEMS TO DISCUSS (FEEDBACK/SUPPORT):

_____

_____

_____

_____

NOTES:_____

_____

_____

_____

FEEDBACK/ACTIONS FOR YOU:

_____

_____

_____

NAME: _____ DATE: _____

ITEMS TO DISCUSS (FEEDBACK/SUPPORT):

_____

_____

_____

_____

NOTES:_____

_____

_____

_____

FEEDBACK/ACTIONS FOR YOU:

_____

_____

_____

1:1 MEETING NOTES
(MEETINGS WITH YOUR REPORTS)

NAME: _____ DATE: _____

ITEMS TO DISCUSS (FEEDBACK/SUPPORT):

_____

_____

_____

_____

NOTES: _____

_____

_____

_____

FEEDBACK/ACTIONS FOR YOU:

_____

_____

_____

NAME: _____ DATE: _____

ITEMS TO DISCUSS (FEEDBACK/SUPPORT):

_____

_____

_____

_____

NOTES: _____

_____

_____

_____

FEEDBACK/ACTIONS FOR YOU:

_____

_____

_____

1:1 MEETING NOTES
(MEETINGS WITH YOUR REPORTS)

NAME: _____ DATE: _____

ITEMS TO DISCUSS (FEEDBACK/SUPPORT):

_____

_____

_____

_____

NOTES: _____

_____

_____

_____

FEEDBACK/ACTIONS FOR YOU:

_____

_____

_____

NAME: _____ DATE: _____

ITEMS TO DISCUSS (FEEDBACK/SUPPORT):

_____

_____

_____

_____

NOTES: _____

_____

_____

_____

FEEDBACK/ACTIONS FOR YOU:

_____

_____

_____

1:1 MEETING NOTES
(MEETINGS WITH YOUR REPORTS)

NAME: _____ DATE: _____

ITEMS TO DISCUSS (FEEDBACK/SUPPORT):
_____
_____
_____
_____

NOTES: _____
_____
_____
_____

FEEDBACK/ACTIONS FOR YOU:
_____
_____
_____

NAME: _____ DATE: _____

ITEMS TO DISCUSS (FEEDBACK/SUPPORT):
_____
_____
_____
_____

NOTES: _____
_____
_____
_____

FEEDBACK/ACTIONS FOR YOU:
_____
_____
_____

1:1 MEETING NOTES
(MEETINGS WITH YOUR REPORTS)

NAME: _____ DATE: _____

ITEMS TO DISCUSS (FEEDBACK/SUPPORT):

_____

_____

_____

_____

NOTES: _____

_____

_____

_____

FEEDBACK/ACTIONS FOR YOU:

_____

_____

_____

NAME: _____ DATE: _____

ITEMS TO DISCUSS (FEEDBACK/SUPPORT):

_____

_____

_____

_____

NOTES: _____

_____

_____

_____

FEEDBACK/ACTIONS FOR YOU:

_____

_____

1:1 MEETING NOTES

(MEETINGS WITH YOUR REPORTS)

NAME: _____ DATE: _____

ITEMS TO DISCUSS (FEEDBACK/SUPPORT):

_____

_____

_____

_____

NOTES: _____

_____

_____

_____

FEEDBACK/ACTIONS FOR YOU:

_____

_____

_____

NAME: _____ DATE: _____

ITEMS TO DISCUSS (FEEDBACK/SUPPORT):

_____

_____

_____

_____

NOTES: _____

_____

_____

_____

FEEDBACK/ACTIONS FOR YOU:

_____

_____

_____

Made in the USA
Coppell, TX
25 October 2022

85279031R00070